Cars

Chris Oxlade

First published 2013 by Kingfisher
an imprint of Macmillan Children's Books
20 New Wharf Road, London N1 9RR
Associated companies throughout the world
www.panmacmillan.com

Series editor: Heather Morris
Literacy consultant: Hilary Horton

ISBN: 978-0-7534-4101-5

9 8 7 6 5 4 3 2 1
1TR/0516/WKT/UG/105MA

A CIP catalogue record for this book is available from the British Library.

Printed in China

Picture credits
The Publisher would like to thank the following for permission to reproduce their
material.
Top = t; Bottom = b; Centre = c; Left = l; Right = r
Cover Shutterstock/Ben Smith, Pages 4 Shutterstock/Zoran Karapancev; 5 Shutterstock/
Ben Jeayes; 6–7 Kingfisher Artbank; 8 Shutterstock/qingqing; 9 Shutterstock/Max Earey;
10 Shutterstock/Ahmad Faizal Yahya; 11 Shutterstock/Walter G Arce; 12 Shutterstock/Alexander
Kosarev; 13 Getty/Daniel Garcia/AFP; 14–15 Kingfisher Artbank; 14b Getty/John Chapple;
16 Shutterstock/Peter Weber; 17 Shutterstock/Christopher Halloran; 18 Kingfisher Artbank;
19 Shutterstock/Pics-xl; 20 Shutterstock/Andrey Armyagov; 21t Shutterstock/Katherine Welles;
21b Getty/NiklasHalle'n/Barcroft Media; 22 Shutterstock/sonya etchison; 23 Corbis/Tim Wright;
24 Shutterstock/Dmitry Vereshchagin; 25 Corbis/Michael Rosenfeld; 26 Corbis/Steven Vidler
Eurasia Press; 27 Shutterstock/Faiz Zaki; 28 Getty/Grey Wood/AFP; 29 Getty/ChinaFotoPress

Contents

What is a car?

A car is a machine that carries people on journeys. We go to school in cars, and we go to the shops in cars. Sometimes we go on holiday in cars.

Cars come in many shapes and sizes. There are tiny cars with space for just two people. These cars are good for driving round town and parking in small spaces. Big cars have seats for six or seven people.

This is a small city car.

Car fact
Today there are more than a thousand million cars in the world.

When people drive to work or school, and when they drive home again, towns and cities are full of cars.

The first cars

The car was invented more than a hundred years ago. The first cars looked different from the cars we travel in today. They looked a bit like horse-drawn carriages. They had big wheels, tiny **engines** and were very slow.

This car was made by a man called Karl Benz. It was the first real car.

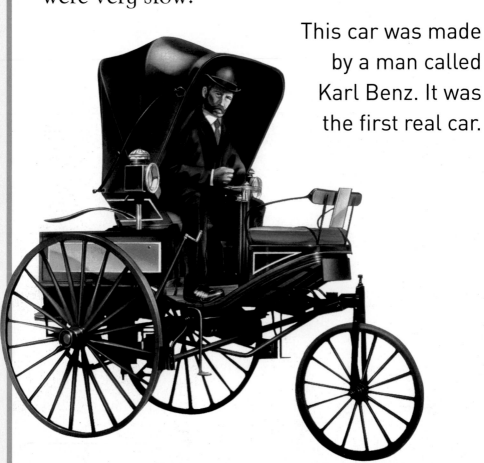

When cars were invented, most roads were rough tracks. There were no petrol stations. Drivers carried cans of petrol and they had to know how to mend their cars.

The Model T Ford was a popular car.

Sports cars

Sports cars are fast and fun to drive. These cars are built for speed and have powerful engines to push them along. They have wide tyres that grip the road as they race round corners. Sports cars have a smooth, rounded shape that helps them go really fast.

This sports car has a folding roof.

Car fact

Supercars can drive at more than 300 kilometres per hour. That's as fast as a speeding express train.

Supercars are the fastest sports cars. Their engines are much more powerful than other sports cars. They are made of special materials so they weigh less than normal sports cars. They go super fast, and are exciting to drive.

Track racers

You can see the thrills and spills of car
racing at a race track. There are races
for sports cars and for special racing cars.
There are even races for family cars.
Crowds of people watch this exciting sport.

Racing car drivers need lots of skill
and lots of practice to drive fast.

Racing drivers sit inside a strong cage that protects them in case they crash. They wear a fireproof suit and a helmet.

Car fact
Racing drivers sometimes stop in a race to put on new tyres. Their team can change all the tyres in just eight seconds.

This is an American track racing car. All four tyres are being changed at once.

Rally racers

Rally cars race along muddy roads and dirt tracks. Sometimes they race through the snow and over frozen lakes. Rally cars need super-strong wheels and tyres.

Rally drivers race along at amazing speeds, sliding round corners and flying over bumps. They even race at night along dark forest tracks.

A **navigator** helps the driver. He tells the driver about **hazards** on the road ahead.

Car fact
The longest rally is the Dakar Rally. The cars travel up to 900 kilometres across the desert each day. The race lasts for two weeks.

Some rally drivers race across deserts. They drive off-road cars over sand dunes, mud and rocks.

The fastest car

What's the fastest car in the world?
The answer is Thrust SSC. The letters
SSC stand for **supersonic** car. In 1997
Thrust SSC reached a speed of 1,228
kilometres per hour. That's an
amazing 340 metres
every second.
Thrust SSC's
driver was Andy
Green. He had
been a fighter
aircraft pilot.

Thrust SSC zooms across the desert.

Car fact
Thrust SSC travels faster than some **jet planes**.

The record for the world's fastest car is called the world land speed record. One day another car will probably go faster than Thrust SSC. Two new cars that might beat Thrust are the Bloodhound SSC and the North American Eagle.

Custom cars

Some car owners make their cars look weird and wonderful. They take off some parts and add new ones, such as mirrors and wheels. They change the shape and paint them with amazing patterns and pictures.

Some custom cars are built for drag racing. They are called dragsters. They race each other along a short track at high speed.

These dragsters are ready to race.

At the start of a race, the drivers spin their wheels to make the tyres sticky. Then, zoom… they're off! Just a few seconds later, the race is over!

Car fact
Drag racers use a parachute to slow down at the end of a race.

Car parts

All cars have an engine. The engine turns
the car's wheels, and the wheels move the
car along. An engine needs **fuel** to make it
work. Most cars use petrol or diesel as fuel.
The fuel goes along a pipe to the engine
and burns inside the engine. This makes
the engine work.

Car fact
All the moving parts of
an engine are covered
in oil. The oil lets the
parts move smoothly.

A car rolls along on wheels. The wheels move up and down as the car goes over bumps. Each wheel has a rubber tyre, which is filled with air. The rubber grips the road and stops the car sliding around.

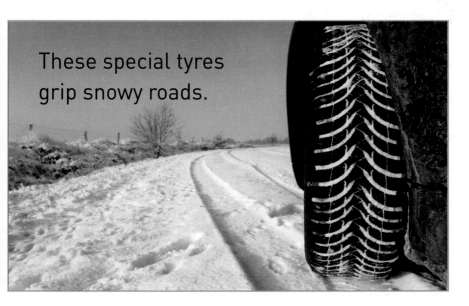

These special tyres
grip snowy roads.

Driving a car

Have you watched someone driving a car? The driver presses pedals to start moving, speed up, slow down or stop. The driver turns the steering wheel to go round corners. Switches near the steering wheel work the lights and the windscreen wipers.

It takes a long time to learn to drive a car. Drivers have to learn how to make the

Left or right?
In some countries cars drive on the left side of the road. In most countries they drive on the right side of the road.

car move along, and how to **steer**. They learn what the signs on the road mean. All drivers have to pass a driving test before they are allowed to drive on their own.

This car has special controls for disabled drivers.

Car safety

Sometimes cars have accidents. Sometimes they bump into each other or they skid off the road. Cars have parts that keep drivers and passengers safe in an accident. Seat belts keep people in their seats. **Airbags** blow up like balloons. They stop people from hitting the windscreen.

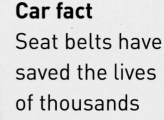

Car fact
Seat belts have saved the lives of thousands of people.

Seat belts go across people's chests and laps.

A crash-test dummy
inside a crashing car

Cars are tested to see how safe they are
in an accident. Scientists smash a car into
a wall or another car to check how strong
the car is. They put a large doll called a
crash-test dummy inside the car to test
the seat belts and airbags.

Making cars

Most cars are made in huge factories. Machines press and fold sheets of metal. The sheets are joined up to make the car's body. This is covered with layers of tough paint.

The body moves through the factory. As it moves, the engine, the seats, the doors and all the other parts are fixed to it. When the car is finished, it is tested to make sure all the parts work properly.

In the factory, people do some jobs and robots do others. Robots can work all day and all night without getting tired.

Car fact
Car makers build more than 50 million new cars every year. That's one-and-a-half cars every second!

Electric cars

Most cars have engines that need petrol or diesel to make them go. Electric cars are moved along by electric **motors**. They have a big battery that works the motor. When the battery runs out of electricity, the driver **recharges** it. Electric cars are quiet, but they can't go very far before their batteries run down.

A hybrid car has both an engine and an electric motor. The engine doesn't turn the wheels. It turns a machine called a **generator**. The generator makes electricity to work the electric motor and also to recharge the batteries. Hybrid cars use much less fuel than cars that only have an engine.

The parts of a hybrid car

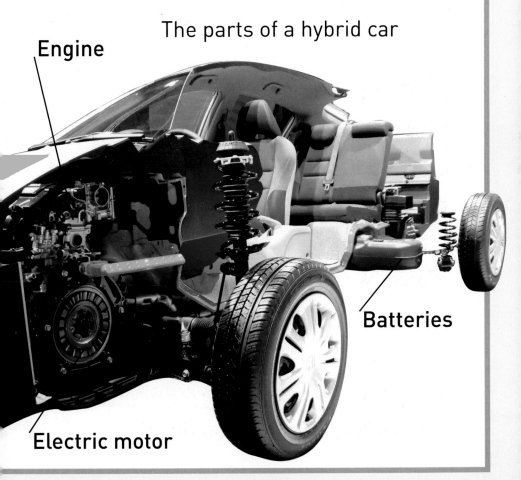

Engine

Batteries

Electric motor

Future cars

Cars are really useful machines, and many people love their cars. But cars harm our planet. Their engines cause **pollution** in the air. In busy cities pollution from cars makes it hard for some people to breathe.

Cars also give out a gas called **carbon dioxide**. This gas is making our planet warmer. It is one of the things causing a problem called **climate change**. Electric cars give out no carbon dioxide. Hybrid cars give

out less pollution
and carbon dioxide
than normal cars.

People enjoy
a car-free
day in China.

The solar
cells on
this car use
energy from
sunshine
to make
electricity for
the engine.

Glossary

airbag A bag that blows up like a balloon to protect a driver and passengers in a car accident.

carbon dioxide A gas given off when things are burnt, for example when cars burn fuel.

climate change Changes that are happening to the patterns of weather around the world, caused by human activities.

crash-test dummy A life-sized doll used to see what might happen to people in a car accident.

engine Part of a car that makes the car move.

fuel A liquid that burns inside an engine.

generator A machine that transforms movement energy into electricity.

hazards Dangers.

jet plane A plane that is pushed along by jet engines.

motor A machine that spins when electricity flows into it, transforming electricity into movement energy.

navigator A person who finds the way from place to place.

passengers People other than the driver who travel in a car.

pollution Waste that humans put into the environment. Gases from car engines are one kind of pollution.

recharge To refill a battery with electricity when the battery has run down.

steer To make a car turn to the right or left, or go straight on.

supersonic Faster than sound travels through the air.

Index